Written by Odile Bombarde
and Claude Moatti
Illustrated by François Place

Specialist adviser: Simon James,
The British Museum

ISBN 1 85103 030 1
First published 1987 in the United Kingdom by
Moonlight Publishing Ltd,
36 Stratford Road, London W8

POCKET • WORLDS

Living in Ancient Rome

Some cities in the world
are thousands of years old...

This city is nearly three thousand years old!

It is Rome, the capital of Italy.
Today, in and around the busy streets, you can see old ruins, like the Coliseum, left over from long ago.
The streets of ancient Rome were once as busy and noisy as the streets of modern Rome are today.

What was it like, living in Rome around the time Christ was born?

The Romans were governed by their Emperor Augustus and Roman power stretched over all the lands around the Mediterranean Sea. Everywhere, in the countries the Romans ruled, you can still find the remains of their buildings, roads, and everyday objects like pots and coins. They have left traces of their lives wherever they settled.

This Roman coin has a picture of Augustus, the first Roman Emperor.
(The writing says 'Augustus Divi F.': 'Augustus God's Son'.)

The Coliseum in Rome, as it looks today

What a din!

During the night, you would hear the wooden wheels of the carts rumbling along the stone roads, and the drivers swearing at the animals and cracking their whips. During the day, crowds of people bustled past. There were so many people living in some parts of Rome that buildings were six or seven storeys high. They often caught fire; the Romans set up one of the earliest fire-brigades. Packed with shops and monuments and all the business of government, Rome attracted people from all over the Empire – traders, teachers, philosophers and fighters.

Roman scales

In the taverns, the men would sit and drink wine.

Men would go to the barber's to be shaved and perfumed.

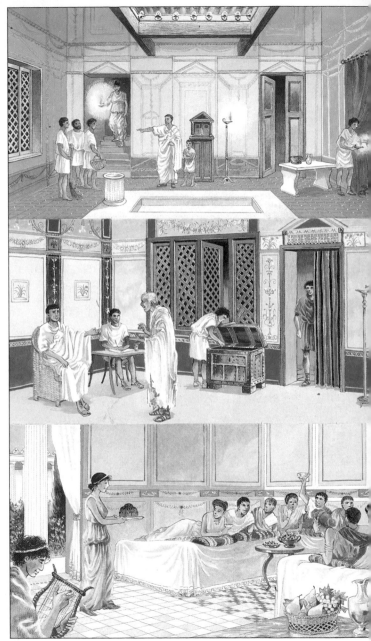

How did a Roman spend his day?

The Roman here was very well off, and lived in a big house. At daybreak, he woke up and had a breakfast of bread and cheese, before giving out the day's money or food to the people he looked after. Slaves did all the housework. The main meal of the day, the **cena**, was in the middle of the afternoon. Often, a lot of friends would be invited to share it. They used to lie on couches, and eat with their fingers. What did they eat? Boiled ostrich, spiced hedgehogs, fried roses... Poorer Romans had simpler meals: bread, olives, grapes and honey. They ate very little meat.

As soon as it was dark, most people went to bed. The most usual lights were oil-lamps, and they were smoky and expensive to run. Only the rich could afford to stay up after dark.

Every house had an altar, where offerings were left for the Lares, the household gods.

11

The mistress of the house had her hair done and her face made up every morning by slaves.

There weren't many Roman houses with bathrooms. Most people just washed in a bowl of water.

How did the Romans dress?

The men wore togas, the women dresses caught up round the waist. Boys wore a locket, a bulla, at their necks as a protective charm.

1, 2. Slaves wearing tunics

3, 4. The master and mistress

The toga was semi-circular and could be draped in different ways.

chool was held in an
lcove, shut off from
he street by a curtain.

Off to school

Only a few boys,
between seven
and fifteen years
old, went to school. They would set off
very early in the morning. A slave went
with each boy to carry his wax tablets
and the sharp stylus used to write on
them. The teacher was often a
foreigner, a Greek. He would punish bad
pupils with a rod called a ferula.

What games did Roman children play?

They had toys such as hoops, wooden
tops, and dolls made of wax or of clay.
They played at jacks... Sometimes they
invented games with nuts, making
them into little carriages to tie to mice.

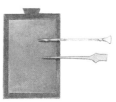

What a schoolboy needed: papyrus rolls — these were the
Roman books — pens and ink-well, a wax tablet, styli.

This is the Forum, the main public meeting-place in Rome.

Most of the buildings here were made of white marble. Augustus added so many important buildings to Rome, in the Forum and elsewhere, that he said: "I found Rome brick and left it marble."

1

There were temples and triumphal arches, and inscriptions to remind Romans of their famous past and their responsibilities for the future.

1. Temple of Jupiter on the Capitol
2. Via Sacra, the 'sacred way' leading to the temples
3. Rostra. Men stood up here to make speeches on the important issues of the day
4. Record office, where all the public records were kept

The baths had different pools, some hot, some warm, some co

Nearly every afternoon, all the well-off Roman men went to the public **baths**. They bathed there and talked with their friends and played games.

It was one of the great pleasures of their lives! The **water** which Rome needed was brought to the city by means of fourteen aqueducts. They carried it to the baths, to the gardens, to the public lavatories, and to the fountains. Water for the houses was fetched in big earthenware pots called amphorae.

The first Roman sewer was built 2,500 years ago and is still used today!

The Romans were great ship-builders.

Rome was the market-place for all the world.

Most things came by sea, in huge merchant ships. Wrecks have been found which had ten thousand amphorae on board. These long clay pots held everything from wine to oil.

Carts weren't so good for carrying things. Whether they had two wheels or four, they were slow, bumpy and expensive to run.

A warehouse

A shop

Ostia was the port of Rome. As soon as a ship arrived there, its cargo was taken off and loaded on to a river boat. These small boats travelled up the River Tiber to the warehouses in Rome, where it was stored.

You could buy anything in Rome, because the whole of the Empire sent its produce there.

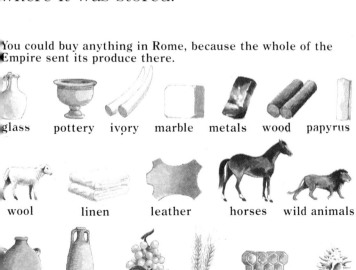

glass   pottery   ivory   marble   metals   wood   papyrus

wool

linen

leather

horses

wild animals

oil

wine

fruit

cereal

honey

murex

In the Italian countryside lots of people were hard at work.

An olive oil press

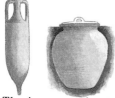

The jars were kept cool, up to their necks in soil.

There were slaves working for their masters, and small farmers working the land for themselves. They grew vines for grapes and wine, and harvested olives for olive oil.

Each big farm had its own flour-mill and bakery.

The Romans used a lot of olive oil; they didn't make butter. They kept herds of goats and sheep. The soil was worked with a simple wooden plough which broke up the soil. It was pulled along by a pair of oxen. Sometimes, in between the vines and the cypress trees, there were beautiful houses, called villas, where rich Romans came to get away from the noise and bustle of the city.

Each chariot team had its own colour and claimed the protection of a particular god: Jupiter for the whites, Neptune the blues, etc. They had their own fans, too, like modern football clubs.

Bread and circuses!

That's what the Roman Emperors gave the people to keep them happy. Almost every other day there would be something to go and watch: chariot races, gladiator fights, plays...

The Romans liked gambling for money with dice.

All the shows were free.
Sometimes there might be
a hundred chariot races held in
a single day. These games were held on
a race-track called the Circus Maximus,
which the chariots had to go round
seven times (it was called a circus
because they went round in a circuit).
Up to 25,000 people could watch and
bet on the chariots as they hurtled along.

Wild animals and men fought together in the amphitheatres.

The biggest amphitheatre of all was the Coliseum. Fifty thousand people could sit all round it on the stone benches. In the centre was a huge arena, with a barrier round the edge to protect the spectators from the wild animals. A canvas roof was stretched over the top in the middle of the day to protect people from the bright sunshine. The amphitheatre could be used for mock sea-battles too; the whole arena was flooded, and real boats brought in to sail on the water.

Underneath the seats were passages along which the animals could be led into the arena, and where all the materials for the different shows could be stored.

The games went on from sunrise to sundown.

Sometimes there were men hiding behind iron grilles, firing arrows at the wild animals. At other times, gladiators fought the animals face to face, with just a spear or a sword against bulls, lions, panthers, tigers... There were animal fights, too: a bear against a bull, or an elephant against a rhinoceros. Perhaps cruellest of all was when the gladiators were made to fight each other. Some gladiators were popular professional fighters, others were slaves or condemned criminals, or poor people attracted by the chance of high wages.

Before the fight, the gladiators would salute the Emperor
and say: "Ave Caesar, morituri te salutant," which means
"Hail Caesar, those who are about to die salute you."

Retiarius   Myrmillo   Samnite

At the end of the fight, the winner waited for the Emperor's
signal. Thumb's down, the loser died; thumb's up, he
lived to   fight another day.

27

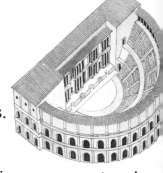

At the back of the theatre was a high wall. It was used for scenery and bounced the actors' voices back towards the audience.

<u>At the theatre</u>, the public could watch comedies or tragedies. Most popular of all, though, were knockabout farces, mimes or pantomimes with music and songs. The first big stone theatre was built at the time of Julius Caesar. If an audience got too noisy, the producer would call for silence: "Slaves must not sit all over the place; nurses must not bring babies with them, and women must laugh silently!"

Actors wore masks to show which characters they were playing. This is Dionysos, god of the theatre.

A comic actor, shown in a mosaic

For a long time, the games were held in honour of the gods. Their gods were very important to the Romans. There were a lot of different ones, but the most important of them was the Father of the Gods, Jupiter. The Romans asked the gods for their protection and help through sacrifices of goats, pigs and bulls. The animals for sacrifice were decorated with garlands of flowers, and then led to the altar where the priest killed them with an axe.

Before a battle, the priest would watch the sacred hens to see how they behaved. If they ate their grain hungrily, it was a good sign.

ave you seen remains of the Roman occupation where
u live, like Hadrian's Wall here, or the triumphal arch below?

rom Spain to Syria, from North Africa
o the borders of Scotland, **the Roman
army conquered a vast Empire**. The
Romans had to set safe boundaries to
heir conquests. The soldiers built
ortified camps everywhere, and
onstructed a huge network of roads so
hat the army could move about
uickly. A lot of the roads
till remain. They usually
o straight from
oint to point.

The soldiers have set
p camp. Now they will
uild solid huts to live in.

The Roman legion at war

There were 310,000 soldiers at the time of Augustus. Half of them were legionaries, well armed foot-soldiers, the rest were cavalry and archers. Here the army is besieging a town. The soldiers have catapults (1) to throw stones and arrows against the defenders, a battering-ram (2) to break down the gate, and a siege-tower (3) and scaling-ladders (4) so that they can climb over the walls and into the town.

The Romans triumphant After a great victory, the Emperor was given a triumph: a procession through Rome.

3. Then followed the animals prepared for sacrifice, and the prisoners of war.

5. He wore special clothes: a purple tunic embroidered with gold, golden sandals, an ivory sceptre and a crown of laurel leaves.

. At the head of the procession came
musicians, then porters carrying all the
booty which had been won, and models
of the towns which had been captured.

. Finally, with officers and soldiers in
front of him and behind him, came the
triumphant Emperor in his chariot.

. Behind him stood a slave holding
over his head a golden crown taken
from a statue of Jupiter. His children
rode with him or on horseback behind.

The Romans live on in our language.

They didn't only leave remains made of stone or metal, they left traces of their language too. Thousands of English words come from Latin, the language the Romans spoke. For example, there's the word 'example' itself, which comes from the Latin *exemplum*. And 'language' comes from the Latin *lingua*. A lot of English people call their house a *villa*, just as the Romans did. The 'pedal' on your bike comes from the Latin word for 'feet', *pedes* ('pedestrian' comes from the same word as well). A 'mile' is called that because it was a thousand (*mille*) paces for a Roman foot-soldier. And 'computer' comes from the Latin word for 'to calculate', *computare*.

The Romans had a story that Rome was founded by Aeneas, a Trojan hero. You can see him here fleeing with his household from Troy after it has been burned by the Greeks.

Pocket Worlds – building up into a child's first encyclopaedia: